Peregrinations
along the
Great Wall

Peregrinations
along the
Great Wall

PEREGRINATIONS ALONG THE GREAT WALL

Author : Cheng Dalin
Text Sub-editor : Wang Guanmin
Executive Editor : Yim Lai Kuen
Translator : Sin-sing Kong
Photographers : Cheng Dalin, Wang Guanmin, Zhang Shuicheng,
Chan Man Hung, Yau Pik Shan, Yang Zuming, Feng Jing,
Liu Wenmin, Yim Lai Kuen, Alfred Ko, He Shiyao,
Wang Wenbo, Hu Weibiao, Liu Kai Tak, Wang Fatang.
Design : Shuttle Production
Publisher : The Commercial Press Ltd, Hong Kong Branch,
4/F., Kiu Ying Bldg., 2D Finnie St., Quarry Bay, Hong Kong.
Distribution Agent : China National Publications Import & Export Corporation,
137 Chaoyangmennei Dajie, Beijing, China.
Color Separation : Goody Color Separation (Scanner) Ltd.
20/F., North Point Ind. Bldg., 499 King's Road, Hong Kong.
Printer : C&C Joint Printing Co., (H.K.) Ltd.
75 Pau Chun Street, Kowloon, Hong Kong.
Edition : First Edition July 1987
© 1987 The Commercial Press Ltd. Hong Kong Branch
ISBN 962 07 5057 8

TABLE OF CONTENTS

Preface

Luo Zhewen

"Never can one be a true man without setting foot on the Great Wall!" To tourists local or from abroad, the Great Wall has always been one of the major tourist attractions of China.

The Great Wall, with its full name in Chinese literally meaning "Long Wall of Ten Thousand Miles", is unparalleled in world architectural history both with regard to its long history and its enormous scale. A number of centuries ago it was already listed as one of the "Seven Wonders of the Medieval World". As reported by the American astronaut Neil Armstrong, the first man to land on the moon, looking back from the moon or from the spaceship, the Great Wall is one of the most conspicuous human constructions on the earth.

The Great Wall is actually much longer than ten thousand Chinese miles (*li*, translated here as [Chinese] mile, is a unit of length roughly corresponding to half a kilometre). Historical records throughout the ages inform us that over twenty feudal states and imperial dynasties have taken part in the building, rebuilding, extension, and renovation of the Great Wall. A rebuilding or an extension does not always follow the former course or take an obvious route. Centuries of building and rebuilding, therefore, have resulted in a Great Wall with sections running crosswise, and with main lines both north and south of the northern border regions. Preliminary investigations reveal that the total length of the various sections of the Great Wall built throughout the ages amounts to over fifty thousand kilometres. The sections built respectively by the Qin, the Han, and the Ming dynasties are each well over ten thousand *li* in length. The Great Wall extends so far and wide that remains of it can be found today in provinces, municipalities, and autonomous regions as diverse as Liaoning Province, Hebei Province, Tianjin Municipality, Beijing Municipality, Shanxi Province, Inner Mongolian Autonomous Region, Shaanxi Province, Ningxia Hui Autonomous Region, Gansu Province, Xinjiang Uygur Autonomous Region, Shandong Province, Henan Province, Hubei Province, and Hunan Province. Just the remains of the Wall within Inner Mongolian Autonomous Region have been found to be of a total length of over fifteen thousand kilometres.

The Great Wall is a massive defence complex extremely

complicated in structure. Its basic design is not a single line, but a whole network. The long wall itself is but one of the constituents of the entire complex; it is accompanied by over a thousand fortified passes, over ten thousand beacon towers, and countless forts and fortresses. Every dynasty in Chinese history paid serious attention to the defence of the Great Wall. High officials, both civil and military, were often sent to take command of the garrisons around the Wall, with a view to improving the defence mechanism. During the Ming dynasty about a million generals and soldiers were always garrisoned around the Great Wall. And these garrisons were organized into an administrative network comprised of nine border regions and eleven garrison towns, each garrison town being commanded by a chief military officer. Extending westward from River Yalüjiang to Jiayuguan Pass and spanning a total distance of over seven thousand kilometres, the Ming Great Wall received its most substantial improvement and reached a new height in its strength under the careful planning of the famous general Qi Jiguang (1528-1587): for the first time it was adequately equipped with parapets, barrier walls, protruding shields, and watchtowers.

What enable the defence posts along the Great Wall and the forts and passes on both sides of the Wall to coordinate so well in their functioning are the beacon towers, known during the Qin and Han dynasties as beacon pavilions or simply beacons, and during the Ming dynasty as smoke mounds. Smoke and fire are utilized as signals — using smoke in the daytime and fire during the night — by which information about enemy attacks can be sent immediately to the various military strongholds, transmitted to the command posts, or even relayed all the way to the capital.

The immense difficulty involved in the building of the Great Wall is astounding. It can be imagined what a great difficulty it must have been to transport bricks each weighing scores of kilograms and stone slabs each over a thousand kilograms up to sites upon steep slopes and cliffs. Thinking of this we cannot but be amazed at and be proud of the industriousness, the wisdom, and the perseverance of our ancestors.

The former stage of history of some two thousand years has passed. States of affairs in which feudal princes struggle to become lord of the land or in which different peoples strive to subdue one another being no longer present, the Great Wall has completely changed its character. Once a device for defence, once an instrument of war, the Great Wall has now become a great pacifying force, a strong bond that holds together people of different nationalities on Chinese soil, Chinese people overseas, and foreign friends from all over the world into a lasting unity.

Foreword

The Great Wall, the greatest monument of ancient Chinese architecture, is a miracle in the architectural history of the world.

In the vast expanse of territories north of the Yangtze River, stretching from Heilongjiang in the east to Xinjiang in the west, the Great Wall makes its way through more than ten provinces, municipalities, and autonomous regions. Relics of the Great Wall can also be found beyond the northern border of China, in the territories of the Soviet Union and the Mongolian People's Republic. The Great Wall covers a total distance of over 50,000 kilometres.

High walls, numerous trenches, thousands of beacon towers and moated forts make up the colossal construction known to us as the Great Wall. These structures were built of whatever material available locally, be it mud, stone, brick, or even a mixture of reeds and sand. It has been estimated that if the materials used in the making of the Great Wall were to be used instead to build a wall measuring five metres in height and one metre in thickness, the wall could possibly circle round the earth more than ten times.

The Great Wall was born of military needs within the Chinese Empire. The five thousand years of Chinese history had been punctuated by numerous wars between different tribes, different races, or between the central government and the local powers.

Remains of the long wall built by the Kingdom of Qi of the Warring States period; in present-day Changqing County in the suburb of Jinan City, Shandong Province

It was among these wars that the Great Wall came to be built, extended, and consolidated.

The age from the 7th to the 5th century B.C. saw the decline of the Zhou dynasty, the rise of the feudal states, and the intensification of the wars between the states. Great numbers of slaves and common people were driven to the battlefields. The trenches, moats, and wooded hills formerly effective as barriers against advancing chariots constituted no obstruction to these new barefoot warriors equipped with arrows and clubs. A new system of defence — high walls coupled with trenches, moats, and beacon towers — therefore came into being.

As far as we can gather from the discovered remains, the portion built by the Kingdom of Qi appears to be the oldest section of the Great Wall. Built in the 5th century B.C., this section of the Wall extends from Changqing County (in the suburb of Jinan City, Shandong Province) in the west to the coastal area of Huangdao District of Qingdao City in the east, making a length of 500 kilometres. Following the example of Qi, the Kingdoms Chu, Wei, Zhao, Yan, and Qin, or even the Kingdom of Zhongshan, founded by a minority race, seemed to vie with one another in constructing their respective sections of the Great Wall. The northern kingdoms of Qin, Zhao, and Yan, in their determination to stop the nomadic tribes like the Huns and the Tartars from advancing southwards, also contributed to the construction of certain northerly sections of the Wall.

After five centuries of wars and annexations, unification was at last brought to the land in 221 B.C. with the founding of the Qin dynasty. The unification had been brought about by the unchallengeable might of the troops under the command of the founder of the new dynasty, who envisaged an empire that would last forever and styled himself "The First Emperor".

Unification means that hereafter the bulk of the construction of the Great Wall would be shifted to the northerly borders.

The North had always been a great stage on which the various minority tribes or races — the Huns, the Tartars, the Turks, the Khitans, the Jürchens, the Mongolians, and the Manchus — took turns to show off their might. Most of these tribes or races were undergoing a transition in their basic social institution, a transition from slavery society to feudal society, when they first appeared on the historical stage to make themselves known. The life style and culture of the Han Chinese had a great attraction for these nomads. The nomadic economy of these people also demanded that they maintain a close contact with the Chinese in the heartland of the empire, and that an intimate relation with the central government of the

Portrait of Qin Shihuang, the founding emperor of the Qin dynasty

empire should be sustained. These nomadic people traded with the Han Chinese, obtained help and support from the lord of the grand empire through entering into marriage relationship with the family of the lord; but there were also occasions when they forced their way into the heartland to loot and plunder. They might even overthrow the central regime and make themselves rulers of China when the oppression from the Chinese rulers had become unbearable.

Rulers of the various dynasties in Chinese history, whether themselves Chinese or not, paid particular attention to the defence work of the North. The belligerent and unpredictable cavalrymen of the northern grasslands made defence problems almost insurmountable. It is under this great demand for an effective defence system that military engineers throughout the ages have learnt how to make the best of natural geographical features and resources in setting up fortifications. The Great Wall is the crowning achievement in this tradition. Walls and beacon towers are located at various strategic points. Fertile soil and sources of freshwater are planned to be within the confines marked by the Wall. Sometimes destructive strategies might be adopted: strategic areas would be turned into wastelands, trapping the enemies in adverse conditions. This is an economical

and effective way of preventing sudden attacks from the grassland raiders. The system of defence centred around the Great Wall has been recognized to be unsurpassed in effectiveness by experts in the art of war in different periods of Chinese history. Starting from the Qin dynasty, not only regimes founded by Han Chinese, like the Qin, the Han, the Sui, the Tang, and the Ming, made efforts to extend or renovate the Great Wall, regimes founded by minor nationalities, like the Northern Wei, the Eastern Wei, the Northern Qi, the Northern Zhou, the Liao, the Jin, and the Qing, also had substantial contribution to the extension and renovation of the Wall. The greatest efforts had been made by the four dynasties of Qin, Han, Jin, and Qing, each having contributed to the building or renovation of over ten thousand *li* (a Chinese unit of length roughly corresponding to half a kilometre) of the Great Wall. It is explainable, therefore, why the full Chinese name of the Wall literally reads "The Long Wall of Ten Thousand *Li*".

The Great Wall of the Qin dynasty took on its present shape after unification had been brought to China proper by the founder of the dynasty, Qin Shihuang. It was constructed under the supervision of Grand General Meng Tian and the crown prince Fusu. Some three hundred thousand men from the army and hundreds of thousands of men from

Marshes lying just outside of the Great Wall of the Han dynasty at the western section of Dunhuang County, Gansu Province

The Great Wall of the Han dynasty at the western section of Dunhuang County had been most strategically located. Natural marshes that would be extremely dangerous to stride through were incorporated into the defence system of the Great Wall. Beautiful as they were to set one's eyes on, these marshes were graveyards for those who dared to set foot on them. On the other hand, those who were on the line of defence behind the wall enjoyed the advantage of having such resources as water, grass, and fertile soil near at hand.

A section of the Great Wall of the Qin dynasty at Guyuan Prefecture, Ningxia Autonomous Region

The Great Wall of the Han dynasty at Chaoge Prefecture, Mongolian Autonomous Region

amongst the common people took part in the construction. It took nine years to complete the Wall by linking together and adding extensions to the northern long walls built by the Kingdoms of Qin, Zhao, and Yan in former times. Running east-west from Liaodong to Lintiao, Gansu, the Qin Great Wall encompasses over ten thousand *li*. It is the first "Long Wall of Ten Thousand *Li*".

The Han Great Wall was mainly constructed during the reign of Emperor Wudi. Beginning from Liaodong in the east, it reaches western Gansu Province, passes through Dunhuang County, and extends across the vast Gobi Desert and desolate marshes until it terminates at Lop Nur, Xinjiang. A number of extra walls were also built; the one furthest north extends into present-day Mongolian People's Republic. The total length of the Han Great Wall amounts to over twenty thousand *li*. This easily marks the Han Wall the longest among its rivals.

The Great Wall of the Jin dynasty is the longest among the long walls built by the dynasties founded by minor nationalities. This "Wall" is in fact a structure predominantly made up of trenches; hence it is also known as "The Boundary Trench of the Jin". It

The Great Wall at Badaling under a blanket of snow

The Great Wall at Mutianyu

is composed of a number of constituent trenches, distributed around the central and eastern parts of the Mongolian Highland, reaching northern Hebei Province in the south and Mongolian People's Republic and the Soviet Union in the north, with a total length of more than ten thousand *li*.

The Ming Great Wall has its starting point by the bank of River Yalüjiang in Liaoning Province; it runs westward until it terminates at Bulongji, just west of Jiayuguan Pass in Gansu Province, making a total length of some fifteen thousand *li*. The Ming dynasty is the last dynasty to have carried out large-scale construction projects with the Great Wall, and the technology employed is the most advanced ever used. The sections of the Wall at Badaling, Mutianyu, Jinshanling, and the passes of Shanhaiguan and Jiayuguan, today among the favourite tourist spots along the Great Wall, can rightly be claimed to be the highlights of the Ming Wall.

What we find along the Great Wall are either high mountains and deep valleys, or vast deserts and boundless grasslands. Taking into consideration the lack of advanced engineering technology and means of transport in former times, we can imagine how great a

The Great Wall at Jinshanling　　　　　**Jiayuguan Pass**

difficulty must have been involved in transporting and fitting into place the enormously large amount of building materials. An astounding quantity of manpower was spent. The Qin and the Han dynasties made it a rule that every man should spend at least a year in his life building or guarding the Wall. In subsequent dynasties cases of conscripting great numbers of peasants to extend or renovate the Wall recurred from time to time. In A.D. 555, the Northern Qi government sent a million and eight hundred thousand people to build a section of the Wall spanning 450 km from Juyongguan Pass to Datong, Shanxi. It was a common practice in different dynasties to drive criminals to the frontiers to consume their labour in wall construction. The millions of soldiers stationed along the Wall also participated in construction work. The sections of the Wall built during mid-Ming and late Ming were completed by soldiers.

Construction work of the Great Wall was organized and supervised on the basis of "contracting by sections". First of all, the officers and engineers in charge of the project would estimate and specify the workload, the time required, and the standards of quality. Then sections of the wall would be assigned, on a contractual basis, to different construction units. On the completion of a section, the officers and engineers would inspect to see if the finished structure met the specified standards. If anything was not up to standard, it would have to be redone, and the construction unit concerned might have to pay a fine — or might even be subjected to corporal punishment if it was during the Qin dynasty. From mid-Ming on construction units were required to put down on tablets the workload, the time needed, and the names of the unit officers; and the tablets had to be buried within the wall or set onto the wall. The brick makers were also required to place their names and the dates of production on the bricks. All this was designed to eliminate any uncertainty in the attribution of responsibility.

An enormous number of casualties had been involved in the building of the Great Wall. According to the *Hanshu* (Standard History of the Han Dynasty), when the Qin Great Wall was built under the command of Grand General Meng Tian, countless men lost their lives, corpses crowded the wilderness, and blood flooded an area stretching across thousands of miles. Li Mengyang, a poet of the Ming dynasty, writes in one of his poems: "This year the order has been given that the Great Wall is to be built; half of the men conscripted now lie dead before the Wall." The legend of Meng-Jiang Nü, a widow said to have brought down a section of the Great Wall with her

A stone tablet, excavated within the site of the Great Wall at Jiayuguan Pass, with an inscription that records how the construction work for this section of the Wall——built during the Jiajing years of the Ming dynasty——was organized

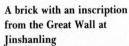

A brick with an inscription from the Great Wall at Jinshanling
The inscription reads: "Made by the Left Regiment of Shandong in the sixth year of Wanli [1578]", indicating when and by whom the bricks for this section of the Wall were made.

tears, is symbolic of the catastrophes connected with the building of the Wall.

But the blood of the builders was not shed for nothing. The Great Wall had an important role to play in Chinese history.

The Great Wall not only protected the economic and cultural developments of the Chinese heartland from external disruptions, it also shielded the Silk Road from various sorts of danger, maintaining free traffic on it for a thousand years. It is via this free passage that silk, paper, and gunpower were transmitted from China to the West, and Western religions, music and dances, as well as wool fabrics and vegetables were transmitted from the opposite direction into China. These exchanges have substantially enriched both the material life and the spiritual life of the Chinese people. The Dunhuang Grottoes and the Maijishan Grottoes in Gansu Province, with the art treasures they contain today still shining with lustre, bear witness to the richness of the cultural activities possible under the aegis of the Great Wall.

The building and guarding of the Great Wall have often formed the core of some grand development projects in northern China. To ensure supplies for the builders and the garrison troops, the Qin government constructed a express passage of 900 km running from norther Shaanxi to Baotou City in Mongolian Autonomous Region. The Ming government developed a sea route linking Shandong Peninsula and Liaodong, and dredged and extended the Grand Canal of the Sui dynasty, making the northern terminus of the Canal just 50 km south of the Great Wall. In tackling the problem of supplies, extensive plans were made for the opening up of wastelands along the Wall by garrison troops and for large-scale construction of irrigation systems; emigration to the neighbouring regions of the Great Wall was enforced or encouraged.

Production and construction along the Great Wall have continued for over two thousand years. This has deep and far-reaching effects on the course of Chinese history. It has facilitated, to say the very least, economic, cultural, and racial assimilation between the North and the South as well as between the East and the West.

Some say that the Great Wall is half a volume of Chinese history; some say that genuine understanding of China cannot be attained without going to the Great Wall. If you want to have a better understanding of China, why don't you come and take a look at the Wall.

A stone mortar found near a watchtower of the Great Wall at Jinshanling
Mortars like this one were carved out of the rocks from the surrounding mountains so as to facilitate the processing of raw foodstuffs for the troops stationed around this section of the Wall.

Chapter 1
The Ming Dynasty and the Great Wall

In 1368, Zhu Yuanzhang overthrew the Yuan dynasty of the Mongols and reinstated Han rule in China with the Ming dynasty. The remnants of the Mongol forces retreated to the Mongolian Highland and founded the Northern Yuan dynasty in opposition to the Ming, awaiting the chance to regain their former status. Zhu Yuanzhang for a number of times sent huge armies into what is present-day Mongolian People's Republic; but owing to the difficulty of maintaining supplies over a long distance, efforts aimed at conquering the Northern Mongols had not met with much success. Because the newly founded dynasty needed stability for economic rehabilitation and political consolidation and could not afford raising large-scale conquering campaigns sustained over long periods of time, Zhu Yanzhang had to resort to a defensive policy. Generals Xu Da and Feng Sheng were ordered to construct long walls and set up fortifications in the north.

By the time Emperor Chengzu, the third emperor of the Ming dynasty, ascended the throne in 1402, the Northern Mongols had split into three groups of powerful tribes, one of which became subject to Ming rule, whereas the remaining two of which, the Oirats and the Tartars, continued to cause troubles around the frontier. In order to unite the whole of China and to strengthen the defence of the north, Emperor Chengzu decided that the emperor himself should not be far away from the front. In 1420, therefore, the capital was transferred to Peking (Beijing). To show his determination the emperor even moved the royal tombs to the new capital, and designated Changling as the site for his own tomb. The emperor himself led five campaigns to curb the Mongols, on one occasion advancing as far north as present-day Soviet borders. He died in 1424 on his return from the fifth campaign. The eventual failure of Emperor Chengzu's attempts to subjugate the Mongols had dissuaded succeeding emperors from taking a similar course of action; and they reverted to the defensive policy of consolidating the Great Wall. Starting from the time of the first emperor, the history of the building and renovation of the Great Wall in the Ming dynasty spans a period of nearly two hundred and seventy years. The Ming certainly surpasses all former dynasties in its technology of building the Great Wall and in the rigorousness of the defence mechanism it demands from the Wall.

The Ming Great Wall constitutes a multi-layer system of defence. Multiple fronts were set up around strategic regions. Series of multiple walls were constructed in Ningxia, Shaanxi, Shanxi, and Hebei. The complex in Shanxi is composed of four constituent walls lying roughly in parallel, the distance between adjacent walls varying from tens to hundreds of kilometres. Passes with fortifications and sets of shorter walls stand formidably at various strategic spots. The valley just dozens of kilometres around Yanmenguan Pass contains twenty-eight walls; a valley twenty kilometres from Mount Badaling (in Beijing Municipality) accommodates four fortresses, the most important of which is the renowned Juyongguan Pass. Different lines of defence are connected by networks of beacon towers and forts, resulting in a formidable defence system.

A large number of troops of the Ming dynasty, amounting to eight or nine hundred thousand men in all, garrisoned the Wall. Nine defence regions, known in those days as "towns" and corresponding to modern military districts, were established in Liaodong, Ji, Xuanfu, Datong, Shanxi, Yansui, Ningxia, and Guyuan respectively. Under each of these garrison towns are the subdivisions of *wei*, or stations, each consisting of 5,600 soldiers; under each station there are camps of 1,200 soldiers, and these camps are subdivided into lesser camps of 120 men each; two banners are under the command of a lesser camp, and lesser banners of ten men each terminate the hierarchical division. Sometimes special subdivisions such as "routes" and "commissions" might be set up under a garrison town in response to particular needs. In mid-Ming the nine towns were combined into three major garrison regions.

The commander-in-chief of a major garrison region, usually a minister or a vice-minister of the Ministry of War, is not only the highest-ranking military officer of the region, but is also the head of the local administrative agency. A garrison town is under the command of a chief military officer and a deputy chief military officer; below there are such positions as assistant regional commander, mobile corps commander, and commandant. Manoeuvres in important wars would be supervised by the grand academician sent directly by the emperor. It can thus be perceived that the army personnel are organized into a closely-knit functioning body with the central government directly on top and an intricate hierarchy of administrative and military agencies below.

Emperor Ch'eng-tsu of the Ming dynasty.

An illustration showing how massive defence walls were constructed in ancient China

A command tablet of the Ming dynasty used by the commander in charge of the troops stationed around the section of the Great Wall at Yongchang County, Gansu Province

A ritual tower at the Dingling Tomb of the Thirteen Tombs
Among the Thirteen Tombs of the Ming Emperors situated in Changping County of Beijing Municipality, the tombs Dingling and Changling are particularly remarkable.

Chapter 2
The Great Wall at the Garrison Region of Jiliao-Baoding

and makes every effort to strengthen its defensive power: walls are built on every strategic mountain that can possibly allow a wall to stand, every passage through the mountains is provided with fortifications; a substantial portion of the wealth of the nation is appropriated for consolidating the walls and forts with stones and bricks. The section of the Great Wall in this major garrison region can be said to be the cream of the whole Wall. Such tourist attractions as the passes of Shanhaiguan, Yiyuankou, Xifengkou, Gubeikou, Zijingguan, and Daomaguan, and sections of the Wall at Jinshanling, Mutianyu, Huanghuazhen, and Badaling, are all to be found here.

The Great Wall at the garrison region of Jiliao-Baoding, which is comprised of the garrison towns of Liaodong and Ji, and the lesser region of Baoding, is an important line of defence shielding the capital and the royal tombs from external dangers.

Peking, the capital of the Ming dynasty, is surrounded in the east by the Bohai Sea, the north by the Yan Mountains, and the west by the Taixing Mountains. East of the Bohai Sea are the original homelands of the various Mongol and Jürchen tribes. The Yan Mountains, part of the Mongolian Highland, stood on the main route through which the Mongols directed their southern raids. Along the Taixing Mountains runs the only passage that goes right through from Shanxi to Peking.

The section of the Great Wall to be garrisoned by the town of Liaodong spans a thousand kilometres east-west from River Yalüjiang to Shanhaiguan Pass. Coupled with Shanhaiguan, the main fortress in the garrison town of Ji, it constitutes the eastern defence line of the capital. The section of the Wall to be garrisoned by Ji rises from Shanhaiguan in the east, snakes over the Yan Mountains, and terminates at Juyongguan Pass in the west, spanning 900 km in total. It is the northern defence line of the capital. The section of the Wall to be garrisoned by Baoding extends westward from Juyongguan, passes through Zijingguan and then turns south, making its way along the Taixing Mountains until it reaches the borders of Hebei and Henan. With a length of 700 km, it functions as the western line of defence of Peking. These three sections combine to make a length of 2,600km; equipped with over five hundred forts and garrisoned by over two hundred and fifty thousand regular soldiers, this is the strongest shield for the capital conceivable. The Ming government considers this garrison region to be the very base of the nation,

Shanhaiguan Pass

Shanhaiguan Pass, located in present-day Shanhaiguan District of Qinhuangdao City, Hebei Province, belonged to the garrison town of Ji during the Ming dynasty. It is the most important pass on the eastern half of the Ming Great Wall. The pass overlooks the Bohai Sea in the south, and leans against the Yan Mountains in the north. A passage of the utmost strategic importance, 10km in width, runs between the sea and the mountain range. This has always been a strongly fortified area ever since the Sui dynasty. In 1381, Xu Da, the Duke of Wei, set up fortifications in this area. From then on a sub-wall, branching off around the Yan Mountains and extending southward up to the seashore, became attached to the Great Wall. The corridor linking the northeast with the central heartland was thus blocked up in the middle. The fortress for this sub-wall was erected as if set against the Great Wall in the east, arising as it were between mountains and seas. It was hence called "Shanhaiguan", literally corresponding to "Mountain-sea Pass". A couplet formerly written on scrolls and hung on the pillars of a renowned hall claims that this is the top-ranking fortress along the Great Wall, and that it occupies a position of unparalleled strategic importance, a key position controlling the access to the two capitals. Xiao Xian, a presented-scholar of 1472 and a well-known calligrapher, has written down on a large horizontal placard the words "The First Fortress Under Heaven" in a most forceful style. Today the placard can still be seen hung high outside a tower at the eastern gate of the fortress.

Shanhaiguan Pass has five constituent forts, integrated with the Great Wall and a number of beacon towers. The fort now open to the public is the principal constituent of the whole complex. This main fort measures 4.3km in perimeter, and occupies an area roughly in the form of a square. It has four gates on its four sides, each originally having a tower on top. Now only the tower on top of the east gate remains. The terrace at the east gate reaches a height of 12m, and the tower above it is 13.7m in height. The tower consists of two storeys. The upper storey is a wooden structure, with painted decorations in Ming style, and the four wing-like corners of the eaves are decorated with ridges in the forms of beasts in different postures. The lower storey is built of brick and wood. The east, the north, and the south sides of the tower have a total of sixty-eight openings for arrows, each with a cover painted as a target with concentric rings. When invaders approach these windows will be opened allowing arrows to be shot out.

The pass is strictly on guard against invasion from every side. The gates on the four sides of the main fort are each shielded with an urn-like fortified enclosure. The urn fortification outside the east gate is further protected by a web-like fortification. Surrounding the main fort is a moat measuring 10m deep and 20m across. To increase the depth of the defence system, a fort of "far-reaching dignity" is set up a kilometre from the east gate. The main fort is also flanked on the north and south sides with wing forts. At the spot where the Great Wall meets the sea there stands a "sea-pacifying" fort, to guard against invaders raiding from the sea. On the Wall are erected such fortifications as Jiaoshanguan, Beishuiguan, and Nanshuiguan. In mid-Ming, when the famous general Qi Jiguang was the commander of the garrison town of Ji, he ordered the building of an extension that protruded the Great Wall over twenty metres into the sea. The protrusion is the well-known "Old Dragon's Head". Built of stone slabs and originally about ten metres high, Old Dragon's Head has long fallen into ruin. At the "sea-pacifying" fort near Old Dragon's Head there still stands a stone tablet inscribed with a phrase of four words meaning "heavens open with a vista of mountains and seas". The characters inscribed are said to have been the handwriting of General Qi.

With the painstaking designs applied to Shanhaiguan by the Ming government during its history of over two centuries, the pass has evolved into a most formidable defence complex. Had it not been the case that Wu Sangui surrendered to the Manchus and let them in through the gates, the Manchus might not have been able to challenge the network of defence laid around the pass.

Today Shanhaiguan is part of the summer resort of Qinhuangdao City. Aside from visiting the old forts and ancient battlefields, tourists who come here may also desire to pay a visit to the Temple of Meng-Jiang Nü outside of Shanhaiguan.

The tale of "Meng-Jiang Nü bringing down a section of the Great Wall with her tears" is one of the four great legends of China. When the Great Wall is being built under the order of Emperor Shihuang of the Qin dynasty, so the legend goes, Meng-Jiang's husband, to whom Meng-Jiang is newly wed, is conscripted into a building regiment. Seeing that her husband does not return after a long time, Meng-Jiang travels a thousand *li* in search of him, until she reaches Shanhaiguan, where she finds that her husband has already died of exhaustion beneath the Wall. Meng-Jiang Nü bursts into tears, and her tears bring down a section of the Wall as long as eight hundred *li*. To protest against the harsh rule of the Qin emperor, Meng-Jiang takes her own life by throwing herself into the sea. The legend has it that the third block of reef at the sea southeast of Meng-Jiang's Temple is the grave of the poor widow.

**A panoramic view of
Shanhaiguan Pass**

A horizontal placard which reads: "The First Pass Under Heaven"

The fort tower at Shanhaiguan Pass, with an old cannon

A tablet inscribed with the words: "Heavens open with a scene of mountains and seas"

The moat surrounding Shanhaiguan Pass

Gigantic rocks used in the construction of the "Old Dragon's Head" at Shanhaiguan Pass

The "Old Dragon's Head", a structure of the Great Wall that protrudes into the sea, is built of massive blocks of granite. Troughs, which are to be filled with molten iron, are cut on the sides of the blocks. On solidification the iron will hold the blocks firmly together.

Laolongtou——"Head of an Aged Dragon"

The Great Wall at Jiaoshanguan Pass, just north of the pass of Shanhaiguan

The statue of Meng-Jiang Nü in the temple that bears her name

The legendary grave of Meng-Jiang Nü

According to the legend the grave of Meng-Jiang Nü is in a certain part of the sea of Bohai, off the coasts of Suizhong County, Liaoning Province. The rocks that mark the watery grave provide a favourite resort for wild geese in autumn; hence such phrases as "an array of wild geese over the grave of Meng-Jiang" has been coined.

Gubeikou and the Great Wall at Jinshanling

The section of the Great Wall at the garrison town of Ji extends westward from Shanhaiguan Pass, snakes over the Yan Mountains, and strides through such passes as Yiyuankou (in Qinhuangdao City, Hebei Province), Xifengkou (in Qianxi County), Malanyu (north of Qingjingling, Zunhua County), and Huangyaguan (in Ji County, Tianjin Municipality) — some 130 passes in all, until it terminates at Gubeikou, a complex of fortifications of colossal importance for the defence of the capital.

The Gubeikou line of defence stretches over a distance of a hundred kilometre, and contains twenty-eight fortified passes. It stands at the throat of an important passage that winds through the Yan Mountains. The passage leads northward onto the Mongolian Highland, goes through Chengde, the summer resort mountain villa of the Qing dynasty, and then finds its way into the northeast of China, where it is only 120km north of the capital. It is, therefore, one of the major routes through which the various tribes on the Mongolian Highland and in the northeast make their headway southward and place Peking under serious threats. There are three such major routes, the other two being around Shanhaiguan and Juyongguan. But whereas the passages connected with these two passes are long and narrow and heavily fortified, hence easy to defend and hard to penetrate, this is not the case with Gubeikou.

Gubeikou is situated in a fault zone dozens of kilometres wide among the Yan Mountains. Most of the mountains within the fault zone have an elevation varying between 400 and 600 metres; their relative heights are generally within the limits of 40 to 100 metres, and they usually have very gentle slopes. River Chao and its tributaries wind about the mountains. Thus rivers and streams as well as gullies and ditches crisscross the fault zone. The presence of numerous small passages among the mountains poses a serious problem for defence.

From the Northern and Southern Dynasties on, there have been continuous efforts to consolidate the walls and fortifications of this area, but without much success. After the founding of the Ming dynasty, the founding emperor ordered Grand General Xu Da to take command of the defence at Gubeikou, to strengthen the fortifications, and to extend the Wall. This, however, proved ineffective in checking the Mongols from advancing south: Gubeikou was more than once overwhelmed, shocking the capital to its roots. The Ming government could do nothing but further consolidate the fortifications at the pass. By 1520s Gubeikou had evolved into a strongly fortified pass. The main fort was built upon the two mountains flanking River Chao in the east and the west, and occupied an area 2km in perimeter. In addition, a large number of beacon towers were set up along the river. In 1550, Gubeikou again fell under Mongolian assaults. A tribe of Tartars bypassed the main fort by making its way through some narrow maintain paths and breaching the Wall. The Tartars plundered around the outskirts of Peking for eight days before they returned swaggering through Gubeikou. In 1554 the same tribe of Tartars raided Gubeikou thrice within a single year.

The falling of Gubeikou time and again greatly disturbed the Ming government. In 1567 Grand Academician Zhang Juzheng, an outstanding politician of the Ming dynasty, transferred Tan Lun and Qi Jiguang, who had been immensely successful in warding off the attacks of Japanese pirates along the southeastern coast, to the garrison region of Jiliao-Baoding. Tan Lun was made Commander-in-chief of the region, and Qi Jiguang was appointed Chief Military Officer. Tan and Qi, together with Liu Yingjie, newly appointed the Grand Coordinator of Shuntian, were entrusted with the task of redefining the garrison divisions within the region and formulating a comprehensive scheme of defence. Under the new arrangement the garrison town of Ji was divided into twelve garrison "routes", to be subsumed under three major regiments. Gubeikou was converted into a "route" and subsumed under the Regiment of Shixia. Under the support of Zhang Juzheng the three new commanders of the region implemented their scheme of large-scale rebuilding of the Great Wall at Jiliao-Baoding Region.

To strengthen the defensive power of the Wall was the chief aim of the rebuilding. Beacon towers were set up at some points of commanding elevation north of the Wall. Slopes on the outward side of the Wall were steepened, and extra fortifications, known as horse barriers, were constructed with blocks of stone. Barrier gates and hollow watchtowers innovative in design were erected around these fortifications. The result was an organically integrated defence complex.

The widespread use of cannons and firearms at that time demanded that the walls and watchtowers had to be built solidly with brick and stone, and that bases for cannons be set up. The rebuilding largely transformed this section of the Great Wall, enabling the region to settle in peace for scores of years. The "Biography of Qi Jiguang" in the *Standard History of the Ming Dynasty* writes of this: "Qi Jiguang commanded the region for sixteen years, constantly building the Wall while strengthening the armed force. Peace was at last brought to the pass at Ji. Qi's successors continued his policy, and for scores of years the region was free of external dangers." A tablet discovered on the Great Wall at Jinshanling contains an inscription that records not only an occasion of the inspection of the Wall by Tan Lun and Qi Jiguang, but also the construction of the Jinshanling Wall at Shandong under the supervision of Qi Jimei, a younger brother of Qi Jiguang.

The Jinshanling Wall is a part of the defence complex centred around Gubeikou. It is situated 5km east of Gubeikou, extending eastward from Longyukou to Capital-in-sight Tower. Five passes of varying sizes and sixty-seven watchtowers in different forms are scattered along its length of 10.5km. As its name suggests, it is built over the Greater and the Lesser Jinshan Mountains. It now lies within the boundaries of Luanping County, Hebei Province.

The Jinshanling Wall is laid out against a wide horizon. Imposing in appearance while rigorous and intricate in its system of defence, it is one of the most outstandingly built sections of the Great Wall.

The Jinshanling Wall is well provided with watchtowers, the average interval between adjacent ones measuring only about 100m, contracting to 50-60 m where the topography causes complications. Qi Jiguang specifies that every watchtower should be within the reach of cannons from an adjacent one; that is to say, adjacent watchtowers should be able to offer mutual support, thus shielding the wall in between from dangers. All the watchtowers are set up at points of commanding elevation. Because the walls slope steeply up towards the watchtowers, terraces have to be built on the walls. On each of these terraces there is a set of shorter walls, about 2.5m high. On these walls there are peepholes and shooting holes. These shorter walls, which shield two thirds of the surface of the main wall, are known as "barrier walls". They constitute a kind of structure unique to the Wall around Gubeikou. In case the enemies succeed in climbing up to the top of the main wall and are about to attack the watchtowers, the guards on the wall may set up lines of defence behind the barrier walls.

The watchtowers at Jinshanling are cast in a great variety of forms; some cubic, some compressed, and some convoluted. They are all in two storeys. The lower storey serves as a lodge for the soldiers and a storeroom for weapons and supplies. Protruding walls are constructed on the outward side of the upper storey, while in the middle of this storey stands a small house known as "scull of the tower", sometimes also called "bed-house", which serves as a shelter or resting place for the soldier on guard. There are arrow openings on the lower storey of the watchtower. The number of such openings varies from tower to tower.

On the Jinshanling Wall there is a watchtower that is outstandingly large. On the terrace on its southern side there is a storehouse. A wall of a hundred metre extends north from this tower along a ridge, until it reaches the confluence of some gullies. At this terminating point there is also a watchtower. A pair of circular beacon towers overlook the confluence. This peculiar watchtower is not only equipped with such defensive devices as barrier walls, it is also shielded with an arc of compound wall on its outward side. On a slope some 60m from the compound wall stands a double fort. The intricate system of defence built around the tower indicates that it is not an ordinary watchtower. It might have been what is known in some historical records as the "Commanding Tower", where the command post for the forefront of defence action is to be found.

Near the eastern end of the Jinshanling Wall a mountain soars steeply towards the sky. The Great Wall climbs up the mountain along the sharp ridge, until it reaches the summit which is nearly a thousand metres above sea level. On the summit stands a watchtower. It is said that looking out from the tower at dawn on a fine autumn day, one may be able to see the lights in Peking; hence the name "Capital-in-sight Tower". The walls built upon the ridge are mostly non-compound in structure. Shooting holes are scattered all over the walls, and shooting can be done in any posture appropriate. Walls of this sort are known as "walls for actual fighting", and can only be found on the Jinshanling Wall.

The Great Wall at Yiyuankou

Remains of the Great Wall at Xifengkou
Xifengkou has been submerged due to latter-day construction of reservoirs. Only a watchtower and the ruins of a section of the Wall remain standing around the barrier gate.

A distant view of the Great
Wall at Gubeikou

Beneath the Great Wall

Jinshanling at sunset

The Great Wall at Jinshanling

The Great Wall at Jinshanling

Looking out from a watchtower

The Great Wall at Jinshanling

A circular beacon tower on a
section of the Great Wall at
Jinshanling

**Capital-in-sight Tower over the
Great Wall at Jinshanling**
Capital-in-sight Tower, built on a
peak some one thousand metres
above sea level at the eastern end
of the Jinshanling Wall, is so
named because it is said that
looking out from the tower light
radiating from the urban districts
of Peking can be seen. As the
watchtower stands on a peak all
four sides of which are steep
slopes or cliffs, it remains an
enigma how its builders managed
to transport the building materials
uphill to the site.

Barrier Wall——an extra dimension in the defence system of the Jinshanling Wall
Barrier walls are erected to guard against the invaders who succeed in climbing up the bulky main wall. An effective network of defence can be set up (and counteroffensive organized) behind these extra walls.

Bombing stones discovered on the Jinshanling Wall
Bombing stones function effectively as a defensive weapon on the Great Wall. As the invaders approach, they will be "bombed" by these stones flung through bombardment holes on the wall.

A carved stone inscription on the Jinshanling Wall
The inscription records an inspection made of this section of the Wall by the Ming officials Qi Jiguang and Tan Lun in 1570.

47

The North Gate of the Capital – The Great Wall at Huanghuazhen and Mutianyu

If the Badaling Wall is well known for its imposing appearance, and the Jinshanling Wall for its intricate design, then the walls at Huanghuazhen and Mutianyu must have impressed their spectators most with their charming scenery.

During the Ming dynasty Huanghuazhen was commonly known as Huanghualu; that is to say, it was on the same level of military division as Gubeikou — the division of *lu* ("route"). The section of the Great Wall at Huanghuazhen spans 90km and contains seventeen fortified passes. It is situated between Juyongguan and Gubeikou, in Huairou County of Beijing Municipality (Peking), just north of the Thirteen Ming Tombs, and is about 80km away from the urban area of the municipality.

The Huanghuazhen Wall functions as a shield for a pass somewhere south of Zhangjiakou. The area around is a strategic spot with high mountains and narrow paths. In A.D. 555 the Wall in this area was renovated and consolidated by the government of the Northern Qi dynasty. During the Yuan dynasty a battalion was founded here. In early Ming Grand General Xu Da renovated this part of the Wall. After Emperor Chengzu had transferred the capital to Peking and moved the Ming Tombs to the new capital, this section of the Wall came to be regarded as the "North Gate of the Capital".

The sections of the Wall around the main fort of Huanghuazhen are all constructed with cubic blocks of granite. The top surface of the main wall, the parapets, and the watchtowers are all built of solid bricks. The result is a strong solid structure that had been ranked as one of the best constructed sections of the Wall during the Ming dynasty, comparable to the Wall at Badaling. Accompanying the steep mountains and the strong wall are verdant foliage and fragrant flowers growing on slopes overlooking the waters beneath. A line of poetry descriptive of the scene goes: "Beneath the formidable fortress there lies a mirror of water."

Mutianyu is a fortress at the western end of the Huanghuazhen Wall. Located some 15km from the main garrison fort, this major fortress on the western wing commands 2,250m of the Wall as well as seventeen watchtowers. The body of this section of the Wall is constructed with stone slabs measuring 8m in height and 4m across on top. The last large-scale renovation of this wall around Mutianyu was completed in 1569 under the supervision of Tan Lun.

The Great Wall at Huanghuacheng
Situated in Huanghuazhen, a town north of the Thirteen Tombs of the Ming Emperors (in the northern suburb of Beijing Municipality), this section of the Great Wall constitutes an important line of defence keeping guard over the Ming Tombs.

The Great Wall at Mutianyu

A shelter house on the Great
Wall at Mutianyu

A distant view of the Great
Wall at Mutianyu

Juyongguan Pass and the Great Wall at Badaling

Juyongguan is a major fortress at the easternmost section of the garrison town of Ji. As a military division at the level of "route", it commands twenty-four forts and 75km of the Wall. The fortress is about 50km north of Peking and some 40km east of Huanghuazhen, located in a valley which forms part of a passage linking Peking and Mount Badaling. The valley, known as the Fortress Gully, is flanked on its two sides by steep slopes and cliffs. Covered with thick forests and interspersed with gigantic rocks and small streams, the Gully was looked upon in former times as an impassable strip of land. Two large characters meaning "natural impassè" have been carved on a cliff near the Badaling Wall.

The Gully is a shortcut to travel from the Mongolian Highland to Peking. It is through this passage that the Jürchens made their way into Peking and drove out the rulers of the Liao dynasty in 1122. It is also through this passage that in 1644 Li Zicheng, the notorious bandit chief, led a swarm of bandits southward to assault the capital and put an end to the Ming dynasty.

The strategic importance of the Fortress Gully has been recognized as early as in the Warring States period. At that time it was one of the eight well charted paths among the Taixing Mountains, and was known as the Secluded Path, or the Path of the Command Post. Somewhat later fortifications were set up in this area. There was a saying that goes: "There are altogether nine impassable passes under heaven, Juyongguan being one of them." When the pass acquired the name "Juyong" cannot be ascertained. Some claim that the name comes as follows. At the time of Emperor Shihuang of the Qin dynasty, a large number of common people are conscripted into regiments for the building of the Wall, and the conscripted men are known as "petit labourers". Some of these petit labourers are sent to the area that is to become the Fortress Gully. From then on that area acquires the name "Juyong", which has the literal meaning "here reside the petit labourers", and together with its fortifications it is called "Juyongguan".

A mural in a tomb of the Eastern Han dynasty (A.D. 25-221) discovered in recent years at Horinger County, Mongolian Autonomous Region, depicts a scene which shows the lord of the tomb passing through the Fortress of Juyongguan. The fortress in the depiction appears to be a wooden structure, which looks very much like a bridge.

Juyongguan Pass had also been known as West Pass, Toll Pass, and the Pass of Ji.

The Pass has a rigorous, formidable system of defence. It is by no means an isolated fortress. Within the Fortress Gully which spans a distance of over 20km, there are series of defence lines. During the Ming dynasty two main forts, two barrier gates, a major fortress, and two walls were built in this gully.

The southern barrier gate of the Fortress Gully is also known as the Gate of Xia. In A.D. 567 the Northern Qis built a long wall that ran all the way from here to Datong, Shanxi. The wall remains as the last line of defence at Juyongguan Pass. On the wall originally stood a fort, now demolished. 7.5km north of the southern barrier gate is one of the main forts of the Pass.

Juyongguan Pass is a peculiar architectural complex spread out all over the Fortress Gully, centring around a main fort that measures 6.5km in perimeter. The whole complex actually extends on its western side up the steep slopes until it reaches the summit. In this way the defence complex not only locks up the gully, it is also in full control of the points of commanding elevation. Most of the walls in the gully have been demolished. The two gates that remain standing in the gully and the ruins of the walls built upon the ridges still give enough suggestions enabling us to reconstruct the grandeur of the architectural complex in our imagination.

4km north of the Pass was originally another main fort known as the Upper Fort. Abandoned in mid-Ming, it has since fallen into ruin.

As for the paths that snake through the Fortress Gully, once they reach the spot around the Upper Fort, they make a sharp turn and meander upwards along a ridge until they reach an elevation of 800m. There they are blocked by a fortress and a massive wall. This is the northern barrier gate, also called the Badaling Gate, and is the fourth line of defence of Juyongguan Pass. There is an explanation for the name "Badaling". Just outside of the gate lies a defence line composed of a fort (a fort at a fork in the road) and an earth-built wall. Beyond the fort the road that leads towards the Mongolian Highland forks into eight directions; hence the name "Bada" ("eight-sides reaching").

The Badaling Wall is a typical section of the Great Wall. Built of stone slabs in its foundation, it is consolidated in its bulk with solid bricks. Measuring 7.8m high and 5m wide on its top, five horses and ten soldiers can march abreast on the top of the wall. There is a watchtower at every interval of 60-70m.

The fortress at Badaling occupies an area of over five thousand square metres. The wall around is roughly 7.5m high and 4m thick. There are gates on the east and west sides. Badaling is the spot of commanding elevation for the whole Juyongguan complex. An ancient saying goes: "What is impassable at Juyongguan Pass lies not on the pass itself, but on Badaling." If Juyongguan can be compared to the gate of the capital, then Badaling ought to be the key to this gate. It should not be surprising, therefore, that we find a placard above the west gate of the fortress which reads: "The outer garrison of Juyongguan", and one above the east gate which reads: "The key to the north gate of the capital".

There are many historical relics in the Fortress Gully. Among them "the Rock for Viewing the Capital" and "the Terrace on which Mu Guiying (a heroine of the Song dynasty) Appointed her Sub-officers" deserve particular mention. But the real gem among the alleged seventy-two relics to be found here is undoubtedly the Cloud Terrace inside the main fort of the pass.

Built during the Yuan dynasty in 1345, the Cloud Terrace was designed to be the foundation of the Pagoda of Thrupath. The central passage of the main fort leads through the archway under the terrace. According to certain investigations, there were originally three lama pagodas on the terrace. The terrace is built entirely of white marble, and the archway is richly decorated with reliefs. On the facade there are such patterns as birds with golden wings, flowers with curled leaves, and the Great Dragon God. Inside the archway there are images of the Four Great Heavenly Kings on the two sides and two thousand Buddha images on the ceiling. All these are exquisite sculptures of the Yuan dynasty. But even more valuable are the inscriptions of two pieces of Buddhist writings in six different languages: Sanskrit, Tibetan, Mongol 'phags-pa, Uighur, Xixia, and Chinese; the two pieces of writings being the "Dharani Sutra" and "Record of the Building of a Pagoda". These inscriptions are invaluable source materials for the study of the languages of the various nationalities in ancient China.

The Cloud Terrace is a treasure house of the architecture, the arts, the culture, and the religions of the Yuan dynasty.

A full view of the three grand audience halls located centrally in the Forbidden City

The Forbidden City, situated within the central districts of Beijing Municipality, is comprised of groups of palaces of the Ming and Qing dynasties. It is the largest and the most complete architectural complex to be found existing in China.

The Qinian Hall of the Temple of Heaven in Peking
This is the hall in which the emperors of the Ming and Qing dynasties offered sacrifices to the gods of heaven and earth.

Juyongguan Pass as depicted in a mural of the Eastern Han dynasty at Narin Ger, Mongolian Autonomous Region

The gate of Juyongguan Pass

A panoramic view of Badaling

The Great Wall meandering among the mountains

The Badaling Wall at dusk

Autumn scene of the Great
Wall

Protruding walls built upon
gigantic rocks

Treading on the Great Wall
with one's shadows

Close-up view of a watchtower

A watchtower

Looking out from a watchtower

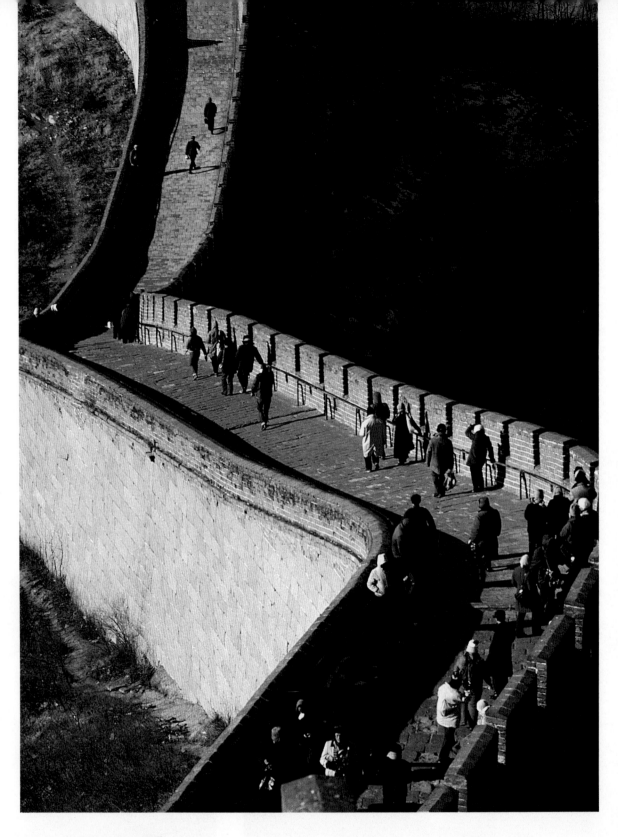

A little scene of the Great Wall

The Badaling Wall covered with snow

Buddhist scripture carved on the wall of the Cloud-Terrace Archway

A relief image of the Ox-eyed Heavenly King of the West on the west wall of the archway of the Cloud Terrace

The Cloud Terrace at Juyongguan Pass

Zijingguan Pass

Juyongguan Pass serves as a line of demarcation both for the Taixing Mountains and the Yan Mountains, and for the garrison town of Ji and Baoding Region. The Taixing Mountains and Baoding Region lie on the eastern side of Juyongguan Pass.

The main line of the Ming Great Wall forks into two branches at Hebei and Shanxi, known respectively as the Inner Wall and the Outer Wall. The Outer Wall begins in the east at Shanhaiguan and turns north when it reaches Mutianyu in Beijing Municipality; it then passes through Dushikou, Zhangjiakou, and Mashikou before it enters Shanxi Province, where it makes its way through Tianzhen County, Yanggao County, Deshengkou (north of Datong City), and Shahukou; it at last joins the Great Wall at Mount Yajiao in Pianguan County. The Inner Wall starts in the east at Mutianyu and extends westward through Juyongguan, Zijingguan, and Daomaguan; then it enters Shanxi and passes through Pingxingguan, Yanmenguan, and Yanggaokou before finally joining the Outer Wall at Pianguan County. The section of the Ming Wall that goes south along the Taixing Mountains is also a part of the Inner Wall.

The Wall at Baoding Region constitutes the eastern section of the Inner Wall, and functions as a shield for the eastern suburb of Beijing Municipality. In case the Outer Wall at Shanxi falls to the enemy, the Baoding Wall would inevitably become the next target of the enemy if they are to advance on Hebei to seize the capital. Along the Baoding Wall there are such important fortresses as Longquanguan, Daomaguan, and Zijingguan, of which Zijingguan, 40km west of Yi County of Hebei Province, is the most formidable and has been termed "The Strongest Fortress in Southern Capital Region".

There are eight important passages running east-west on the Taixing Mountains. These passages are known as "tracks" and Zijingguan is an old fortress on the Seventh Track, or the Track of Puyin. The fortress was called Wuruanguan, Zizhuangguan, and Jinboguan in former times, and acquired its present name during the Song dynasty because there were many Chinese redbud trees (*zijing*) in its vicinity. Juyongguan, Zijingguan, and Daomaguan are the three famous "Inner Passes" of the Ming Great Wall, with Juyong in the north, Daoma in the south, and Zijing lying in between.

The main fort of Zijingguan Pass is roughly 4km in perimeter, and there were originally eight gates along the perimeter. What had once been an imposing building now lies in ruins; only the archways of the gates remain. The north gate is the best preserved of all the gates. Above its archway we can still see seven large characters written by Fu Guangzhai in 1589; they read "Zijingguan" and "Rivers and mountains urge us on like a grindstone". Above the archway of the west gate are four characters, engraved in 1589, making up the phrase "Purple Pass and Golden Fort".

The Great Wall of the Ming
dynasty upon the Taixing
Mountains

Zijingguan Pass

Chapter 3
The Great Wall at the Garrison Region of Xuanda-Shanxi

The garrison region of Xuanda-Shanxi is comprised of the garrison town of Xuanfu in northern Hebei Province, the garrison town of Datong in northern Shanxi Province, and the garrison town of Shanxi in central Shanxi Province.

The section of the Great Wall under the command of Xuanfu and Datong constitutes part of the outer line of the Ming Great Wall. Spanning over a thousand kilometres, the Xuanda Wall serves to protect the section of the Inner Wall at the garrison towns of Ji and Shanxi from immediate external dangers, and may be considered to be an outer line of defence for the capital. During the Ming dynasty not a few momentous wars were fought around this region. In 1449, five hundred thousand soldiers of the Ming army met with almost total annihilation at Camp Tumubao (present-day Huailai County, Hebei) in Xuanfu; and Emperor Yingzong was taken captive by the Oirat Mongols. It was only with the utmost exertion of the forces of resistance under the command of Yu Qian, Vice-minister of the Ministry of War, that the capital was saved from falling into the hands of the enemy. This is the "Tumu Incident" well known in Chinese history.

Xuanfu and Datong are in the neighbourhood of the grazing fields of the Mongols, and are also only a short distance away from Hohhot, where the nobles of the Tartar Mongols used to reside. The area around the two garrison towns, therefore, has long been the marketplace where trade between the races or tribes inside and outside of China proper is conducted. Zhangjiakou, Mashikou, Deshengkou, Shahukou, as well as Datong, were well-known centres of trade in former times.

Datong City, an acknowledged historical town, became an important garrison town along the Great Wall as early as 5th-3rd century B.C. Today a wealth of historical relics can be found in the city; among them are the Yungang Grottoes, the Upper and Lower Huayan Temples, Shanhua Temple and the Wall of Nine Dragons.

Mount Heng and Mount Guanling, which run east-west across central-northern Shanxi Province, serve as a natural boundary for the garrison towns of Shanxi and Datong. High and imposing and at the same time endowed with a charming gracefulness, Mount Heng is one of the five great mountain ranges of China, the "Northern Range" among the five. Mount Wutai in the range is one of the four great "Buddhist Mountains" of China. The family of temples on Mount Wutai and the remarkably constructed Airborne Temple (Xuankong Si) are all located within the Heng Mountain Range.

The western section of the Inner Wall of the Ming dynasty is built upon Mount Heng and Mount Guanling. Encompassing a distance of some 400 km, it is commanded by the garrison town of Shanxi, and is equipped with such fortresses as Niangziguan, Pingxingguan, Yanmenguan, and Pianguan.

Niangziguan is termed "The Ninth Pass of the Great Wall". The name "Niangzi" ("woman") comes from a legend, according to which Princess Pingyang of the Tang dynasty once led a corps of woman soldiers to stand in defence of the pass. While the legend is still widely told, it seems to have been somehow eclipsed by a historical event associated with a neighbouring pass: the decisive victory that the Eighth Route Army have over the Japanese in their first encounter around Pingxingguan Pass.

The Great Wall of the Ming dynasty at Zhangjiakou

Dajingmen Gate at Zhangjiakou
This gate was connected to the Great Wall at a most strategic point, and was, apart from being an important passage, a centre where the different peoples traded with one another.

Reliefs on the roof of a
Yungang grotto

The giant Buddha statue at
Yungang Grottoes, Datong,
Shanxi

Reliefs inside the Temple of
the Five Pagodas at Hohhot,
Mongolian Autonomous Region

The Nadam fair of the Mongols

Xuankong Temple, in Hunyuan County, Shanxi
This temple is built upon the west cliff of the pass of Jinlongkou, beneath the Hengshan Mountains, the great mountain range of the North.

Morning upon Mount Wutaishan

Situated in Wutai County (Shanxi Province), Mount Wutaishan is one of the four celebrated "Buddhist Mountains" in China.

The east gate of Pingxingguan Pass

This important pass on the Inner Great Wall of the Ming dynasty is located 62 km north-east of the capital town of Fanshi County, Shanxi.

The gate of Niangziguan Pass
Located 45 km north-east of the
capital town of Pingding County
(Shanxi Province) and formerly
known as Weizeguan, this is an
important barrier controlling the
passage to Shanxi, and is one of
the most celebrated passes of the
Great Wall.

Daizhou and Yanmenguan Pass

Daixian County was known in former times as Daizhou. The county capital has since the Han dynasty been an important garrison on the defence line of Mount Heng. The county is known in histories as "the commanding access to the entire Jin Region", and "a weighty spot in the midst of the Three Passes". Taking control of it means taking control of the passage for advancing south from northern Shanxi to the central heartland. During the Ming dynasty Daizhou commanded Wutai County, Fanshi County, and Guo County in present-day Shanxi Province. The command posts for such strategic passes as Pingxingguan and Yanmenguan were all to be found within the ancient county capital of Daizhou.

At the central district of the county capital is Drum Tower, also called Frontier-pacifying Tower (Bianjing Tower). High on the facade of the tower are hung two placards which read, respectively: "The First Tower around Yanmenguan Pass", and "Resounding Name Heard Far and Wide". On the rear face of the tower we find another placard with the words "Mighty Prowess Overwhelming the Three Passes". These words and phrases mean no exaggeration. The tower is extraordinary just with regard to its height. With an overall height of 39.3m, it is 14 m higher than the main tower of Shanhaiguan Pass. East of this Drum Tower stands its counterpart — Bell Tower, about 20m high. If any sign of danger is perceived around the frontier, both drums and bells will sound, and the garrison troops will gather together and prepare themselves for fighting.

Yanmenguan Pass, as its name may indicate, is located on Mount Yanmenshan, which is 12.5 km north of the ancient county capital of Daizhou. Mount Yanmen, formerly known as Mount Gouzhu, has an elevation of 2057m at its summit. The only passage across the mountain is a deep narrow gully, called the "West Track". It is said that when the wild geese return·to the north in spring, they are unable to fly over Mount Gouzhu and have to go through the gully, hence the gully comes to be called "Yanmen" (i.e., Gate for Wild Geese"). The strategic importance of this impassable barrier has long been recognized: during the Warring States period Gouzhu Pass was one of the "Nine Great Passes Under Heaven".

The existing main fort of Yanmenguan Pass was built in 1374. The fort is 1km in perimeter, and has an urn-like barrier wall in addition to its east and west gates. Three large characters — "Yan-men-guan" — are inscribed above the gate of the urn-wall; and on the two sides of the gate is a couplet which reads: "A triangularly framed, strategically unrivalled piece of land; a pass that stands out dignifiedly as the first among The Nine". Terms like "Heavenly Endowed Impasse" and "Earth-born Advantages" can be found inscribed on the horizontal tablets of the east gate and the west gate respectively.

The northern opening of the gully is blocked by the new Guangwu Fortress, which was once a barracks during the Ming dynasty. A ruined fortress, walls along the ridges on the two wings, together with a number of densely distributed beacon towers bear witness to the countless battles that were fought mercilessly here. At the base of the mountain, some 2.5km west of the new Guangwu Fortress, stands a very well preserved old fortress — the old Guangwu Fortress. This old fort was built during the Jin dynasty (1115-1234). On one occasion the Jürchens seized upon this stronghold as a field headquarters in confrontation with the Song troops which were just a thousand metres south in a fort built upon a slope.

North of the two Guangwu fortresses are a great number of graves, amounting roughly to a thousand. The relics excavated from these graves appear to indicate that all those buried here were generals or soldiers. There are no gravestones to inform us of the names and deeds of these heroes. But legendary tales about Yang Ye and his sons, national heroes of the Song dynasty, are widespread around this district.

During the ninth century, Yanmenguan Pass was the main battlefield between the Song dynasty and the Liao Kingdom of the Khitans. The Wooden Pagoda in the capital town of Ying County, just northeast of Yanmenguan, was built by the Khitans. It serves both as a religious monument and as a watchtower. The repeated defeats of the Song army seemed to indicate that an able commander was needed. It was under such a demand that Yang Ye was appointed Governor of Daizhou Prefecture and entrusted with the task of guarding Yangmenguan Pass.

In 980, a few thousand cavalrymen under the command of Yang Ye inflicted a serious defeat on a Khitan army of a hundred thousand men in the gully of Mount Yanmen. This was an overwhelming victory; the Grand General of the Khitan army and the husband of the Khitan princess were killed. Thereafter Yang Ye repeatedly showed his might in subduing the Khitans. This earned him the title "Invincible Yang" among the Khitan army.

In 985 the Song army met with defeat in a northward campaign. Yang Ye was ordered to retreat to cover the evacuation of the common people, and was thwarted in his plan for a counteroffensive by oppositions from the chief commander Pan Mei and a superintendent sent by the emperor. Yang was taken captive at Jinshatan around Yanmenguan Pass and starved to death. His eldest son also lost his life in the battle. But the other sons and the grandsons of Yang Ye persisted in their efforts to hold the Khitans in check; and they are known to posterity as the "Generals of the Yang Family". Among them the most outstanding was Yang Yanzhao, the youngest son of Yang Ye, or the legendary "Yang Sixth".

The Yang Generals and their heroic deeds have been devotedly remembered by posterity. Commemorative temples and monuments have been set up in many places. The best preserved of all is the ancestral temple of the Yang family at Lutijian Village, Shanxi. All the villagers of this village have "Yang" as their surname, and are alleged to be the descendants of General Yang Ye.

The Great Wall beyond Yanmenguan Pass

Yanmenguan Pass
This pass, also known as Xixingguan, is built half way up on Mount Yanmenshan, and is some 20 km north-west away from the capital town of Daixian County (Shanxi Province). It is known together with Ningwuguan and Pianguan as "The Three Inner Passes" of the Great Wall.

Bianjing Tower at Yanmenguan Pass

The old Guangwu Fortress

Statues of the famous warriors of the Yang Family
The Yang warriors of the Northern Song dynasty are well known for guarding the region around Yanmenguan Pass against foreign invaders. These statues can be found in the ancestral temple of the Yang Family.

The Wooden Pagoda in Yingxian County, Shanxi
The pagoda, constructed in 1056 and located in Buddha-hall Temple in Yingxian, was originally called the Pagoda of Gautama Siddartha. With a height of 67.13 m, this is the largest and the oldest pagoda-styled structure constructed with wood now existing in China.

Chapter 4

The Great Wall at the Garrison Region of Shaanxi-Sanbian

Shaanxi-Sanbian Region is the westernmost garrison region along the Great Wall of the Ming dynasty. Included within the boundary of this region are the garrison towns of Yulin (or Yansui), Ningxia, Shaanxi (or Guyuan), and Gansu, and the six guard areas west of Jiayuguan Pass (reaching as far as Dunhuang of Gansu and Kumul of Xinjiang). This vast area of territories corresponds to present-day northern Shaanxi, Ningxia Autonomous Region, Qinghai Province, and Kumul (Hami) Prefecture of Xinjiang.

The region has been an area where people of different nationalities come together since very early days. In ancient times it was inhabited by such races and tribes as the Huns, the proto-Tibetans, the Tanguts, and the Mongols. Today it provides the dwelling places for such minority nationalities as the Tibetans, the Hui, the Tu, the Dongxiang, the Yugurs, the Kazaks, the Mongols, the Manchus, the Salars, and the Bonans.

The region forms part of the only passage for travelling from Shaanxi to the Mongolian Highland and to the Western Borders. Apart from its strategic importance, the region is richly endowed with natural resources like forests and grazing areas. Since the Qin and Han dynasties countless battles have been fought in the ceaseless strife to gain possession of the area. And during the dynasties Qin, Han, Sui, Tang, Ming, and Qing efforts were made to rebuild or extend the Great Wall at this region.

In early Ming dynasty, due to the great pressure exerted by the Mongol tribes, and due to some strategic blunders made by the Ming government, the natural barriers provided by the Yellow River were given up and the major defence line was transferred inland. In mid-Ming, the various Mongol tribes crossed the Yellow River and made their way into northern Shaanxi and Ningxia, in the Ordos bend of the Yellow River. Thence frequent raids were made eastward on Datong, and southward on Guyuan.

Some of the tribes even crossed the Hexi Corridor and joined force with some other nomadic tribes in the Qinghai area south of the Qilian Mountains, awaiting the chance to raise a major campaign. In response to such an adverse state of affairs, the Ming government attempted a large-scale construction of the Great Wall at Shaanxi and Sanbian in 1470. Because the natural barrier along the Yellow River had fallen into the hands of the enemies, and because moving the main defence line further inland means abandoning the grasslands, the fertile soil, and the sources of water in the Ordos bend of the Yellow River to the Mongols, the Great Wall at the garrison towns of Yulin, Ningxia, and Guyuan could only be built along the margins of deserts, Gobi areas, and loess plateaux. In order to sever the connection between the Mongol tribes and the Qinghai tribes, and to shield the passage to the Western Borders and its accompanying oases from dangers, the Great Wall at the garrison town of Gansu was built alongside the Hexi Corridor.

Largely conditioned by the complicated topography, the dry climate, and the lack of building materials in Shaanxi-Sanbian Region, the Great Wall at this region is characteristically irregular and intricate in structure: it is discontinuous, sometimes lying crosswise, and with many multiple lines. However, being built of stone blocks and rammed loess, it is extremely strong and enduring.

The Wall at Shaanxi-Sanbian consists of two main lines. The northern line begins in the east at Fugu County, by the bank of the Yellow River at northern Shaanxi; it extends westward through Yulin, Jingbian, and Dingbian, and enters Yanchi County of Ningxia; thence, after passing through Yinchuan City, it goes south along the Helan Mountains, going through Qingtong Gorge en route, and continues west at Zhongwei County, eventually entering Gansu Province at Jingtai County; it then enters Hexi Corridor at Gulang County; proceeding along the base of the Qilian Mountains and passing through Wuwei, Shandan, Zhangyi, and Jiuquan, it at last (at long last!) terminates at Jiayuguan Pass. The southern line starts at Xiamaguan Pass in Guyuan, Ningxia; it passes through Jingda County, Lanzhou City, Tianzhu Tibetan Autonomous Prefecture, and finally joins the northern line at Gulang County, Gansu. The Shaanxi-Sanbian Wall reaches a length of three thousand kilometres, and has two hundred and fifty thousand soldiers around in garrison, as its highest record has it.

A distant view of Zhenbei Tower
This beacon tower on the Great Wall of the Ming dynasty is situated 7.5 km north of the capital town of Yulin County, Shaanxi Province. As the enemies approach, the guards will light a beacon on the tower, signalling the troops stationed nearby to gather together for defence.

Ruins of Tongwan City of the ancient Kingdom of Daxia, in present-day Jingbian
The site is situated on the northern bank of Wuding River on the borders of Shaanxi Province and Mongolian Autonomous Region. It is known that in A.D. 413 Helian-bobo, the chief of a tribe of Huns, sent a hundred thousand of his tribesmen to build a capital for their kingdom of Daxia.

The Great Wall at Dingbian, Shaanxi

The Salt Lake at Dingbian

The Great Wall of the Ming
dynasty at Sanguankou, beneath
Mount Helan, Ningxia

Women and children of the
Hui nationality beneath the
Great Wall at Yinchuan,
Ningxia

The Zhongwei section of the
Great Wall at Ningxia extends
to the bank of the Yellow River

Grazing areas at Yinchuan

The One Hundred and Eight Pagodas on Mount Xiakou at the Qingtong Gorge, Ningxia
Built on a steep slope overlooking the Yellow River, these pagodas are arranged in twelve horizontal rows: the number in each row varies according to the sequence of odd numbers, increasing from top to bottom and hence resulting in a triangular complex. This is the only large-scale complex of old pagodas to be found in China.

Crossing the Yellow River on a raft made of sheepskin

The Great Wall at Tianzhu,
Gansu

The Great Wall at Wuwei,
Gansu

Tibetan girls at Tianzhu

The Great Wall at Shandan,
Gansu

The pagoda of the Temple of Wooden Pagoda in Zhangye, Gansu

The temple is also known as Wanshousi (Temple of Longevity). First built during the Sui dynasty (A. D. 581-618), the existing structure is the result of a renovation done in 1926. The pagoda is constructed with brick and wood, in nine storeys, with a height of 32.8 m.

Autumn scene of the Qilian Mountains

The range forms the southern flank of the Hexi Corridor, with an average elevation of over 4,500 m. More than three thousand glaciers can be found among the mountains, and the rich vegetation around the mid-levels of the mountains provides abundant resources for cattle rearing. In the thick forests there are rare birds and beasts of various kinds, like snow cocks and antelopes.

Jiuquan Park, Gansu
Jiuquan, literally meaning "Spring of Wine", was originally called Jinquan ("Golden Spring"). A limpid spring, it acquired its present name on the occasion when the eminent Han general Huo Qubing was awarded a jug of wine by Emperor Wudi: Huo poured the wine into the spring to share it with those under his command. The pond in Jiuquan Park has its source in the spring.

Jiayuguan Pass

Situated at Jiayuguan, which is 7 km northwest of Jiayuguan City in Gansu, Jiayuguan Pass is the last fortress at the west end of the Ming Great Wall. South of the pass soar the snow-clad Qilian Mountains; and north of it loom the Black Mountains, laden with layers and layers of dark rocks. Complementing this scene are vast stretches of Gobi areas in the West. The pass stands on a corridor leading towards the Western Borders. The ancient corridor, well known as the "Silk Road", is today eclipsed by the Gansu-Xinjiang Highway and Railway. The setting up of five massive barriers at this district by the Han government has set the example of fortifying the pass for succeeding dynasties.

The existing fortications at Jiayuguan Pass were first built in 1372 by Feng Sheng, Grand General for External Campaigns, and were brought to perfection in 1574.

Jiayuguan has been acclaimed as "The Strongest Fortress under Heaven". With a perimeter of only 733 m, it is not impressive in terms of its size; its strength lies instead in the intricacy of its defence system and in the imposing appearance of the whole structure.

On a piece of land with an area of some thirty-three thousand square metres stands the whole architectural complex of the pass, with an inner fort, an outer fort, a web-like barrier wall, an urn-like barrier wall, a command post for the itinerant officer, a temple for the warrior-god, a pavilion for the scholar-god, and a terrace for public functions, built layer upon layer and screen after screen. A fort tower is built respectively over the front gate, Rouyuan Gate, and Guanghua Gate. The one over the front gate was burnt down long ago. The two existing towers are both 17m high, and both are three-storeyed. The lowest storey is built of brick and wood, while the upper two storeys are wooden structures. The roofs of the towers are covered with glazed tiles in green; and all the ridgepoles and beams are carved and painted. The whole structure appears colourful and magnificent. The section of the Wall around Jiayuguan Pass is built of rammed loess or sun-dried mud bricks. The inner wall is 4 m high, its outer side being shielded by a brick-stacked wall of a height of 1.7 m. On the brick wall are shooting holes and peepholes. A corner tower is built upon each of the four corners of the inner fort. The two corners of the west web-barrier are even equipped with arrow-shooting towers.

The front gate of Jiayuguan Pass faces west. On the horizontal tablet above its archway are the three characters "Jia-yu-guan". On the stretches of Gobi areas outside the west gate stands a stele with the words: "The Strongest Fortress Under Heaven", in four characters. Certain archives inform us that there was originally a large horizontal placard with the same words (though in six characters instead of four) hanging on the facade of the tower over the front gate. It was burnt to ashes together with the tower.

Built of rammed loess and measuring 50 km in length and 4 m in height, the section of the Great Wall commanded by Jiayuguan Pass reaches as far south as the Qilian Mountains, extends north as far as the Black Mountains, and to the east joins the Wall at Hexi Corridor.

It is said that in the construction of the forts at Jiayuguan Pass a precise plan for the use of building materials was laid down. When the construction was completed, only one brick was left. The brick was eventually placed on the eaves at the rear of the tower at the "Gate of Report Submission" of the west urn-barrier. There, seen by everyone but could not be reached by anyone, the brick stands as a reminder of the ingenious planning of the builders.

Today, apart from being a tourist resort, Jiayuguan City is a modernized industrial city where iron and steel are produced. Among the tourist attractions are not only the old forts at the pass, but also the celebrated cliff paintings on the Black Mountains and murals on individual bricks in a tomb of the Eastern Han dynasty.

A panoramic view of Jiayuguan Pass

The tower on the right stands over Rouyuanmen Gate. On the left we have Guanghuamen Gate and its tower. Beyond Guanghuamen we have an urn-wall, which is part of the main fort. Beyond the urn-wall stands Guandi Temple, Temple for the Warrior-god. Also in sight is a shrine for the Taoist god who presides over such matters as scholarly honour and official rank. The distant mountains south of the main fort are the Qilian Mountains.

Ornaments on the eaves of a
watchtower

A tablet which reads: " The
Strongest Fortress Under
Heaven "

Sloping horse-track at Guanghuamen Gate

The Great Wall on the Gobi Desert as viewed at a distance from the south-western corner of the main fort of Jiayuguan

Rouyuanmen Gate

The "Last Brick" on the eaves of the rear wall of the tower at Huijimen Gate

Jiayuguan Pass bathed in evening glow

Why Jiayuguan Pass is built here is that, aside from the strategic reason, the natural environment around this region affords ideal living conditions for the troops stationed here. Beyond the east gate of the pass there are nine springs which ensure an ample supply of fresh water for the troops. In the picture we can see a pool where water from the various spings is collected.

The Corner Tower at Jiayuguan
Pass

A section of the Great Wall of the Han dynasty, near Jiayuguan Pass, built of alternating layers of reeds and stone chips

What is remarkable about the building of the Great Wall in ancient China is that the builders utilized whatever material that was available locally; hence some sections of the Wall were constructed with rammed loess, some with stone, and some even with reeds and twigs of poplar. From mid-Ming on cannons and firearms gradually replaced arrows and lances as the main types of weapon used in storming or defending the Great Wall, with the consequence that sections of the Wall that were of strategic importance came to be built chiefly of brick and stone.

A beacon tower near Jiayuguan Pass

The massive earth-built structure seen in the picture is a beacon tower, upon which signals can be sent by firing cannons or hoisting flags. The bottom part is a hollow structure where beacons are lit.

A tomb of the Wei-Jin period with murals inside, in the vicinity of Jiayuguan Pass
The tomb is situated 20 km north–east of the capital town of Jiayuguan, on the part of the Gobi Desert around Xincheng. The murals inside are remarkable. Mostly miniature works painted on individual bricks and with a few large–scale ones, these murals depict the various aspects of everyday life : we see people engaged in farm work, hunting, cooking, and picnicking.

Cliff paintings on Mount Heishan (Black Mountains)
Over thirty paintings of this sort can be found scattered on the cliffs of the gorge of Heishan, north of Jiayuguan Pass. The scenes are usually depictions of military training and hunting. No traces of agricultural life are found depicted, and such weapons as swords and spears are also absent from the depictions. These paintings are most probably early cultural remains of such nomadic peoples as the Tanguts, the Yuezhis (who spoke an Iranian dialect), and the Huns.

Chapter 5
Dunhuang, Yumenguan Pass, and Yangguan Pass

Dunhuang County is situated around the westernmost section of the Hexi Corridor in Gansu Province. Established by Emperor Wudi as one of the four prefectures west of the central basin of the Yellow River, it has a long history of over two thousand years.

In order to crush the Huns and to open up the Western Borders, Emperor Wudi raised a series of major campaigns against the Huns during 121-100 B.C., and at the same time a major passage that leads towards the Western Borders, the famous "Silk Road" as we call it today, was opened. To ensure the passage against seizure by barbarians, the Great Wall was extended alongside the Hexi Corridor to Yanze (Lop Nur in present-day Xinjiang Uygur Autonomous Region), and the four prefectures of Wuwei, Zhangyi, Jiuquan, and Dunhuang were established successively along the Corridor. The prefecture of Dunhuang, as soon as it was established in 111 B.C., became the commanding access to the Silk Road, the pivot for cultural exchange between China and the West, and an important military post along the Great Wall of the Han dynasty. The historical monuments now existing within the territories of Dunhuang, like the Mogao Grottoes, the Western Thousand-Buddhas Cave, the Han Great Wall, Yangguan Pass, and Yumenguan Pass, together with the large quantity of priceless historical relics unearthed from within the territories, bear witness to the glorious history of this ancient prefecture.

Both Yumenguan and Yangguan are well-known passes on the Han Great Wall. They are also important gates on the Silk Road: Yangguan is the entrance for the South Road of the Silk Road while Yumenguan is the entrance for the North Road.

Located among stretches of Gobi areas some 80km northwest of Dunhuang County, Yumenguan is also known as Lesser Fanpan. The site of the fortress appears roughly as a square: measuring 24 m east-west and 26.4 m north-south. The fortress walls, 9.7 m in height, are all built by having loess rammed in between large boards. A gate can be found respectively on the west wall and north wall. North of the fortress passes a thruway running east-west, this being a part of the remains of the Silk Road. The Han Great Wall lies just four or five metres north of the fortress. After passing through Yumenguan the Great Wall makes it way southwest through marshes, lakes, pools of alkaline salts, and extensive stretches of Gobi areas, until it finally reaches Lop Nur. The Great Wall around this region is peculiarly constructed with alternate layers of reeds (or branches of willow and poplar) and sand. The well preserved sections stand up to a height of four metres. It is amazing that a wall of such a nature manages so well to withstand the attacks of winds and rains for over two thousand years. On the inner side of the Wall, beacon towers can be found at an interval of just a few kilometres. Most of these towers are 6-7m high, but some rise to a height of over 10 m and are very imposing in appearance. Houses and courtyards and other living facilities can be found around some of the towers. In 1979, over a thousand and a hundred inscribed bamboo strips and more than three hundred items of other historical relics were unearthed among the remains of one of the beacon towers. Among the relics is a piece of paper which predates the commonly recognized date of invention of the paper by Cai Lun (A.D. ?-121) by more than a century.

20km east of Yanmenguan Pass is a huge depot called Dafangpan (Greater Fangpan) or Helun Fort.

A section of the Wall found to the south of Yumenguan Fortress leads towards the Pass of Yangguan. The old fortress of Yanguan, now buried under shifting sands, was located on Gudongtan some 70km southwest of Dunhuang County. Remains of buildings and a large quantity of relics can still be seen among the shifting sands. On Mount Dundun north of the sands a beacon station of the Han dynasty has been preserved. Similar beacon stations and a large number of Han tombs can also be found south of the sands. Although Yangguan Fortress has fallen into ruin, many tourists, probably among whom many men of letters, still come here to sense a sense of history incarnated in the scenes around. Standing in front of the shifting sands, they may talk about things past and present, and some may like to chant the Tang poem "Song of Weicheng":

In the City of Wei morning rain wets the
floating dust.
Verdant is the lodge and fresh are the willows.
O take my advice, have one more goblet of
wine.

For, once you are west of Yangguan, no old
 friends of yours will be around.

**A mural of the Tang dynasty in
Dunhuang**

111

The Mogao Grottoes of Dunhuang

The Mogao Grottoes, 25 km south-east of the county capital of Dunhuang, stand as a veritable treasure of ancient art works. With the earliest ones built around A. D. 366, the four hundred and ninety-two grottoes have preserved numerous murals and works of sculpture from such diverse dynastic periods as the Northern Wei, the Western Wei, the Northern Zhou, the Sui, the Tang, the Five Dynasties, the Song, the Xixia, and the Yuan.

Stakes in the form of a human face, excavated from a beacon tower on a section of the Great Wall of the Han dynasty, in the western suburb of Dunhuang County

Stakes of this form are usually buried under certain buildings as a means of driving away evil spirits.

A torch of the Han dynasty

The torch, to be lit to give a signal, is unearthed at a beacon tower of the Han dynasty, situated west of Dunhuang. Essentially a bunch of reeds, it has a length of 2.3 m.

A mound of the Qing dynasty, located north-east of the county capital of Dunhuang

It had been a prevalent opinion among modern scholars that the Qing dynasty added practically nothing to the Great Wall. In recent years, however, sections of new wall and beacon towers built during the Qing dynasty, as well as stelae recording efforts made during the Qing dynasty to extend and renovate the Great Wall, have been found in various places along the Wall, as in Shandong, Shanxi, Gansu, and Hebei. Records about Qing efforts in extending and renovating the Wall can also be found in some local gazetteers and non-standard histories.

The Spring of Crescent Moon
Situated among the mountains and rivers around the northern base of Mount Mingshan, Dunhuang, this is a limpid spring with the shape of a crescent. The spring is surrounded on all sides by dunes. Sand blown into the air by wind invariably passes over the spring and never falls into it. For this reason the miraculous scene of having a spring inside a desert has remained intact for thousands of years.

A beacon tower at Yangguan Pass

The beacon tower of the Han dynasty at Yangguan stands amidst vast stretches of sand on the Gobi Desert. Nearby is a verdant oasis. In the background are the Qilian Mountains clad in snow. Surely this is a most fantastic scenery in a desert?

Ruins of Shouchang City, near Yangguan Pass

6 km west of Yangguan Pass lie the ruins of Shouchang City of the Tang dynasty. Numerous historical relics can be found among the ruins. The kind of thing most commonly encountered is the pieces for the game of *go*. According to some records, the *go* pieces made in Shouchang were well known as articles of tribute.

119

Yumenguan Pass

It is through here, so it is claimed, that jade from Hetian was introduced into the heartland of China, hence the name Yumen (Gate of Jade). Beneath the northern slope of the Wall there is a broad carriage track which runs in the south-east direction, this being a historic passage for post communications as well as general transport between the peoples of China proper and the Western Borders.

Remains of the Great Wall of the Han dynasty beyond the Yumenguan Pass

The section of the Han Great Wall beyond the Yumenguan Pass is complicated in structure and intricate in its system of defence. There are an outer wall and an inner wall. The outer wall is high and thick whereas the inner one is somewhat lower and thinner. Between the two walls there is a ditch covered with a layer of fine sand. Footprints or traces will certainly be left on the sand if any human or horse tread through the channel. The ditch was known as the "Heavenly Field" during the Han dynasty.

Combs and beads unearthed at a beacon tower of the Han dynasty
The presence of these women's articles indicates that aside from the guards themselves their family members might also have stayed with them in the beacon towers.

Bundles of faggot left unused at a beacon tower of the Han dynasty
Bundles of faggot were used during the Han dynasty as a signalling device in the various beacon towers along the Great Wall. Different numbers of bundles signify varying numbers of invading troops. Reeds, poplar branches, and willow twigs can all be used as the faggot.

Dafangpan City outside Yumenguan Pass
Built in the Han dynasty, from the Han to the Wei-Jin period this was a supplies depot for the western front which was just beyond Yumenguan.

Map showing the
Locations of
the Great Wall

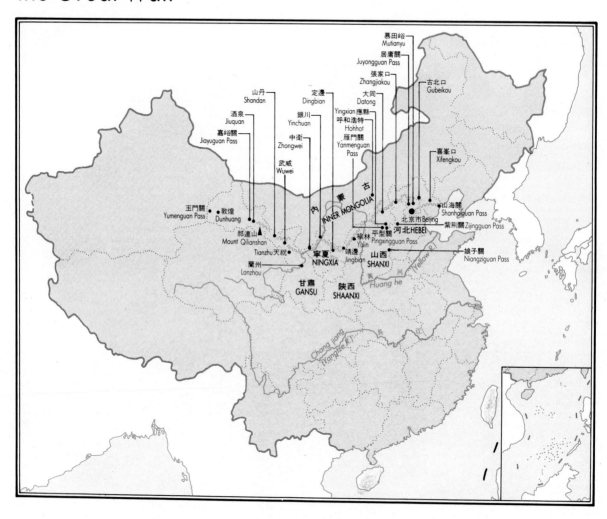

山丹
Shandan

定邊
Dingbian

慕田峪
Mutianyu

居庸關
Juyongguan Pass

張家口
Zhangjiakou

古北口
Gubeikou

酒泉
Jiuquan

銀川
Yinchuan

大同
Datong

嘉峪關
Jiayuguan Pass

中衛
Zhongwei

應縣
Yingxian

呼和浩特
Hohhot

武威
Wuwei

雁門關
Yanmenguan Pass

喜峯口
Xifengkou

玉門關
Yumenguan Pass

敦煌
Dunhuang

祁連山
Mount Qilianshan

內 蒙 古
INNER MONGOLIA

山海關
Shanhaiguan Pass

北京市 Beijing

天祝
Tianzhu

紫荊關 Zijingguan Pass

河北 HEBEI

寧夏
NINGXIA

榆林
Yulin

平型關
Pingxingguan Pass

蘭州
Lanzhou

靖邊
Jingbian

山西
SHANXI

娘子關
Niangziguan Pass

甘肅
GANSU

陝西
SHAANXI

黄 河
Huang he

Chang Jiang
(Yangtze R.)

長 江

Huang he
(Yellow R.)

A Brief Chronology of Chinese History

Xia dynasty		ca. 21 c.B.C.– ca. 16 c.B.C.
Shang dynasty		ca. 16 c.B.C.– ca. 1066 B.C.
Zhou dynasty	**Western Zhou**	ca. 1066 B.C. – 771 B.C.
	Eastern Zhou **Spring and** **Autumn period** **Warring States** **period**	770 B.C. – 256 B.C. 770 B.C. – 476 B.C. 475 B.C. – 221 B.C.
Qin dynasty		221 B.C. – 206 B.C.
Han dynasty		206 B.C. – A.D. 220
Wei-Jin period and Northern & Southern Dynasties		220 – 581
Sui dynasty		581 – 618
Tang dynasty		618 – 907
Five Dynasties/Ten Kingdoms		907 – 979
Song dynasty		960 – 1279
Liao dynasty		916 – 1125
Xixia dynasty		1038 – 1227
Jin dynasty		1115 – 1234
Yuan dynasty		1279 – 1368
Ming dynasty		1368 – 1644
Qing dynasty		1644 – 1911